Congressional Research Service

Informing the legislative debate since 1914 _____

Protection of Trade Secrets: Overview of Current Law and Legislation

Brian T. Yeh
Legislative Attorney

September 5, 2014

Congressional Research Service

7-5700

www.crs.gov

R43714

Summary

A trade secret is confidential, commercially valuable information that provides a company with a competitive advantage, such as customer lists, methods of production, marketing strategies, pricing information, and chemical formulae. (Well-known examples of trade secrets include the formula for Coca-Cola, the recipe for Kentucky Fried Chicken, and the algorithm used by Google's search engine.) To succeed in the global marketplace, U.S. firms depend upon their trade secrets, which increasingly are becoming their most valuable intangible assets.

However, U.S. companies annually suffer billions of dollars in losses due to the theft of their trade secrets by employees, corporate competitors, and even foreign governments. Stealing trade secrets has increasingly involved the use of cyberspace, advanced computer technologies, and mobile communication devices, thus making the theft relatively anonymous and difficult to detect. The Chinese and Russian governments have been particularly active and persistent perpetrators of economic espionage with respect to U.S. trade secrets and proprietary information.

In contrast to other types of intellectual property (trademarks, patents, and copyrights) that are governed primarily by federal law, trade secret protection is primarily a matter of state law. Thus, trade secret owners have more limited legal recourse when their rights are violated. State law provides trade secret owners with the power to file civil lawsuits against misappropriators. A federal criminal statute, the Economic Espionage Act (EEA), allows U.S. Attorneys to prosecute anyone who engages in "economic espionage" or the "theft of trade secrets." The EEA's "economic espionage" provision punishes those who misappropriate trade secrets with the intent or knowledge that the offense will benefit a foreign government, instrumentality, or agent. The EEA's "theft of trade secrets" prohibition is of more general application, involving the intentional theft of a trade secret related to a product or service used in or intended for use in interstate or foreign commerce, with the intent or knowledge that such action will injure the trade secret owner. In addition to criminal enforcement of the statute, the EEA authorizes the Attorney General to bring a civil action to obtain injunctive relief against any violation of the EEA.

However, because the U.S. Department of Justice and its Federal Bureau of Investigation have limited investigative and prosecutorial resources, as well as competing enforcement priorities, some observers assert that the federal government cannot adequately protect U.S. trade secrets from domestic and foreign threats. They have urged Congress to adopt a comprehensive, federal trade secret law in order to promote uniformity in trade secret law throughout the United States and to more effectively deal with trade secret theft that crosses state and international borders (a challenging problem for state courts to address). Among other things, they support the establishment of a federal civil cause of action for trade secret misappropriation, to allow U.S. companies to obtain monetary and injunctive relief when their trade secret assets are stolen.

Several bills have been introduced in the 113th Congress related to trade secret misappropriation, including S. 884 (Deter Cyber Theft Act); H.R. 2281, S. 1111 (Cyber Economic Espionage Accountability Act); S. 1770 (Future of American Innovation and Research (FAIR) Act of 2013); H.R. 2466 (Private Right of Action Against Theft of Trade Secrets Act of 2013); S. 2384 (Deter Cyber Theft Act of 2014); S. 2267 (Defend Trade Secrets Act of 2014); H.Res. 643; H.R. 5103 (Chinese Communist Economic Espionage Sanctions Act); and H.R. 5233 (Trade Secrets Protection Act of 2014). As of the date of this report, none of these proposals has been enacted.

Contents

Contacts

Introduction[1]

U.S. corporations face a "growing and persistent threat" by individuals, rival companies, and foreign governments that seek to steal some of their most valuable intangible assets—their trade secrets.[2] The tools, tactics, and methods used by such perpetrators vary widely but increasingly have involved the use of cyberspace and sophisticated technologies that "mak[e] it possible for malicious actors, whether they are corrupted insiders or foreign intelligence services (FIS), to quickly steal and transfer massive quantities of data while remaining anonymous and hard to detect."[3] As Attorney General Eric Holder has opined,

> There are only two categories of companies affected by trade-secret theft: those that know they've been compromised and those that don't know yet. ... A hacker in China can acquire source code from a software company in Virginia without leaving his or her desk.[4]

Globalization has been cited as a major contributor to the increased incidents of trade secret theft:

> In many ways, trade-secret theft is a foreseeable outgrowth of expanding international markets. When large multinational companies expand their overseas operations, they almost inevitably face challenges related to supply accountability and protection against such theft. Their foreign manufacturing operations and joint-venture partners require customer lists, internal standards, manufacturing processes, information on sources of goods, recipes, and production and sales strategies in order to carry out their operational responsibilities. Each new piece of information that is sent overseas opens a company's supply chain and puts its valuable [intellectual property] at risk.[5]

Several hearings have been held[6] and many legislative proposals have been introduced in the 113th Congress, demonstrating the significant congressional interest in reducing the problems of trade secret theft and economic espionage that U.S. businesses currently face. This report provides an overview of existing federal, state, and international laws governing trade secret

---

[1] Portions of this report have been borrowed and adapted from CRS Report RL34109, *Intellectual Property Rights Violations: Federal Civil Remedies and Criminal Penalties Related to Copyrights, Trademarks, and Patents*, by Brian T. Yeh; CRS Report R41391, *The Role of Trade Secrets in Innovation Policy*, by John R. Thomas; and CRS Report R42681, *Stealing Trade Secrets and Economic Espionage: An Overview of 18 U.S.C. 1831 and 1832*, by Charles Doyle.

[2] Office of the National Counterintelligence Executive, *Foreign Spies Stealing US Economic Secrets in Cyberspace*, October 2011, at i, *available at* http://www.ncix.gov/publications/reports/fecie_all/ Foreign_Economic_Collection_2011.pdf.

[3] *Id.*

[4] Siobhan Gorman and Jared A. Favole, *U.S. Ups Ante for Spying on Firms*, WALL ST. JOURNAL, February 21, 2013 (reproducing a statement made by Attorney General Holder at a White House conference).

[5] *The Report of the Commission on the Theft of American Intellectual Property*, at 41 (May 2013), *available at* http://www.ipcommission.org/report/IP_Commission_Report_052213.pdf. This commission is a private, bipartisan initiative led by former U.S. Director of National Intelligence Dennis Blair and former U.S. Ambassador to China Jon Huntsman.

[6] *Cyber Espionage and the Theft of U.S. Intellectual Property and Technology: Hearings Before the House Energy & Commerce Comm., Subcomm. on Oversight and Investigations*, 113th Cong. 1st Sess. (2013); *Economic Espionage and Trade Secret Theft: Are Our Laws Adequate for Today's Threats?: Hearings Before the Senate Judiciary Comm., Subcomm. on Crime and Terrorism*, 113th Cong. 2d Sess. (2014); *Trade Secrets: Promoting and Protecting American Innovation, Competitiveness and Market Access in Foreign Markets: Hearings Before the House Judiciary Comm., Subcomm. on Courts, Intellectual Property and Internet*, 113th Cong. 2d Sess. (2014).

protection, describes the limitations of these legal regimes, and reviews pending legislation intended to address such deficiencies.

Background

Definition of a Trade Secret

U.S. trade secret law protects secret, valuable business information from theft and espionage. While it has been said that an "exact definition of a trade secret is not possible,"[7] a trade secret generally consists of confidential, commercially valuable information.[8] One U.S. federal court has described trade secrets as follows:

> A trade secret is really just a piece of information (such as a customer list, or a method of production, or a secret formula for a soft drink) that the holder tries to keep secret by executing confidentiality agreements with employees and others and by hiding the information from outsiders by means of fences, safes, encryption, and other means of concealment, so that the only way the secret can be unmasked is by a breach of contract or a tort.[9]

Whether information qualifies as a "trade secret" under federal or state law is a question of fact that may be determined by a jury.[10] A jury may consider several factors in assessing whether certain material is a trade secret, including the following:

- the extent to which the information is known outside of the company;

- the extent to which it is known by employees and others involved in the company;

- the extent of measures taken by the company to guard the secrecy of the information;

- the value of the information to the company and to its competitors;

- the amount of effort or money expended by the company in developing the information; and

- the ease or difficulty with which the information could be properly acquired or duplicated by others.[11]

Eligible Subject Matter and Acquisition of Rights

The U.S. Supreme Court has explained that for subject matter to be protected as a trade secret, the material must meet minimal standards of novelty and inventiveness to avoid extending trade

---

[7] Restatement (First) of Torts §757, comment b.

[8] Uniform Trade Secrets Act §1(4).

[9] ConFold Pac. v. Polaris Indus., 433 F.3d 952, 959 (7th Cir. 2006) (citations omitted).

[10] 4-15 ROGER M. MILGRIM, MILGRIM ON TRADE SECRETS §15.01.

[11] Restatement (First) of Torts §757, comment b.

secret protection to matters of general or common knowledge in the industry in which it is used.[12] In addition, the Supreme Court has held that a person can have a property interest in a trade secret (protected by the Taking Clause of the Fifth Amendment), although "[b]ecause of the intangible nature of a trade secret, the extent of the property right therein is defined by the extent to which the owner of the secret protects his interest from disclosure to others."[13] Therefore, companies may acquire a protectable trade secret property right by putting into place reasonable measures to maintain the confidentiality of certain business information "that is sufficiently valuable ... to afford an actual or potential economic advantage over others."[14] This expansive standard means that trade secret protection could be available to a wide range of proprietary information and technologies that companies rely on to give them an economic advantage over their competitors, including customer lists, methods of production, marketing strategies, pricing information, and chemical formulae.

Duration of Protection

Trade secret protection may extend indefinitely, lasting as long as the subject matter of the trade secret is commercially valuable and is kept confidential.[15] However, the trade secret status of information may be lost if the information is accidentally or intentionally disclosed by anyone.[16] Once a trade secret has been exposed to the public, its protected character is lost and cannot later be retrieved.[17] However, disclosures of trade secrets to third parties for certain limited reasons do *not* waive trade secret protections, so long as the trade secret owner took reasonable measures to maintain its secrecy before and during disclosure, such as requiring non-disclosure or confidentiality agreements from each recipient of confidential information.[18]

Misappropriation

Misappropriation of a trade secret is a tort that may occur in several ways. One is when an individual acquires the trade secret through improper means, such as theft, bribery, misrepresentation, or espionage.[19] Another is when the individual uses or discloses the trade secret through a breach of confidence. For example, an employee might switch jobs and then disclose his previous employer's trade secrets in violation of a confidentiality agreement.[20] Finally, a trade secret may be misappropriated if it is used or disclosed with knowledge that the

---

[12] Kewanee Oil Co. v. Bicron Corp., 416 U.S. 470, 476 (1974)("[S]ome novelty will be required, if merely because that which does not possess novelty is usually known; secrecy, in the context of trade secrets, thus implies at least minimal novelty."); *see also* Ruckelshaus v. Monsanto Co., 467 U.S. 986, 1002 (1984)("Information that is public knowledge or that is generally known in an industry cannot be a trade secret.").

[13] *Ruckelshaus*, 467 U.S. at 1002.

[14] Restatement (Third) of Unfair Competition §39.

[15] United States v. Dubilier Condenser Corp., 289 U.S. 178, 186 (1933) (explaining that rather than seek patent protection, an inventor "may keep his invention secret and reap its fruits indefinitely.").

[16] *See* Religious Tech. Ctr. v. Netcom On-Line Communication Servs., 923 F. Supp. 1231, 1256 (N.D. Cal. 1995).

[17] In re Remington Arms Co., 952 F.2d 1029, 1033 (8th Cir. 1991).

[18] 1-1 ROGER MILGRIM, MILGRIM ON TRADE SECRETS §1.04.

[19] Restatement (Third) of Unfair Competition §40 (1994).

[20] *See* Jennifer Brockett, *Protecting Intellectual Property During Layoffs*, 32 LOS ANGELES LAWYER (April 2009).

trade secret had been acquired improperly or through mistake. A person who uses information that he knows to have been stolen by another is therefore also guilty of misappropriation.[21]

It is not a violation of trade secret law for another party to independently develop the subject matter of a trade secret, or for a party to analyze publicly available products or information in order to discover the secret information.[22] In addition, "reverse engineering," which involves "starting with the known product and working backward to divine the process which aided in its development or manufacture," is not considered an improper means of acquiring the subject matter of another's trade secret.[23]

Misappropriation of a trade secret may be enjoined by a court and the defendant may also be liable for compensatory and punitive damages.[24]

Trade Secrets As a Form of Intellectual Property

Intellectual property encompasses a broad range of intangible property, including the following four categories of subject matter: (1) original artistic and literary works of authorship, such as motion pictures, books, art, photographs, music, and sound recordings (protected by copyright law); (2) symbols, names, colors, sounds, and words that distinguish commercially offered goods and services (protected by trademark law); (3) inventions of processes, machines, manufactures, and compositions of matter that are useful, new, and nonobvious (protected by patent law); and (4) confidential and proprietary business information (protected by trade secrets law). Federal law grants certain exclusive rights to the owners of patents, trademarks, and copyrights and provides remedies in the event that those rights are violated (an act referred to as an infringement).[25] Owners of these three types of intellectual property may enforce their rights by bringing a lawsuit against an alleged infringer in federal court. The U.S. Department of Justice may also criminally prosecute particularly egregious violators of the copyright and trademark laws[26] in order to impose greater punishment and possibly deter other would-be violators. (The Patent Act only provides civil remedies in the event of patent infringement.[27])

In contrast to the other three types of intellectual property that are governed primarily by federal law, trade secrets are primarily governed under state law,[28] and thus owners of trade secrets have more limited legal recourse when their rights are violated by others. State law provides trade secret owners with the power to file civil lawsuits against those who misappropriate trade secrets. Federal law allows U.S. Attorneys to prosecute such offenders but does not currently give trade

---

[21] Restatement (Third) of Unfair Competition §40 (1994).

[22] *Id.* at §43.

[23] *Kewanee Oil Co.,* 416 U.S. at 476.

[24] Restatement (Third) of Unfair Competition §§44, 45.

[25] For a comprehensive description, *see* CRS Report RL34109, *Intellectual Property Rights Violations: Federal Civil Remedies and Criminal Penalties Related to Copyrights, Trademarks, and Patents,* by Brian T. Yeh.

[26] For copyright, 17 U.S.C. §506, 18 U.S.C. §2319; for trademark, 18 U.S.C. §2320.

[27] 35 U.S.C. §281.

[28] The U.S. Supreme Court in *Kewanee Oil Co. v. Bicron Corp.,* 416 U.S. 470 (1974), held that state trade secret laws are not preempted by either the Patent Clause of the U.S. Constitution (Article I, §8, cl. 8) or the federal patent statute (35 U.S.C. §§101 et seq.) Although both trade secret law and patent law protect certain kinds of information, the two fields of law are distinct. For a detailed comparison of patent law and trade secret law, *see* CRS Report R41391, *The Role of Trade Secrets in Innovation Policy,* by John R. Thomas.

secret owners a private right of action in federal court against parties that have engaged in trade secret theft.

Purpose of Trade Secret Law and Comparison to Patent Law

Trade secret law serves as the primary alternative to the patent system,[29] granting inventors proprietary rights to particular technologies, processes, designs, or formula that may not be able to satisfy the rigorous statutory standards for patentability. Companies may choose to maintain an invention as a trade secret rather than obtain a patent because their trade secret rights are not restricted to a limited number of years—unlike patent protection, which lasts less than 20 years and upon expiration, thrusts the invention into the public domain. In addition, trade secret protection is far easier, quicker, and cheaper to obtain (immediately receiving legal protection upon a company taking reasonable efforts to maintain the secrecy of valuable business information), compared to the complicated, lengthy, and expensive process of acquiring a patent, which can take several years and requires the involvement of a federal government agency, the U.S. Patent & Trademark Office. However, obtaining patent protection may be more appropriate in certain instances, such as when a technology is difficult to maintain as a secret because competitors could easily reverse-engineer or independently discover it.

The U.S. Supreme Court has explained that the purpose of trade secret law is to provide companies with incentives to innovate and develop valuable information that may not be patentable:

> Trade secret law will encourage invention in areas where patent law does not reach, and will prompt the independent innovator to proceed with the discovery and exploitation of his invention. Competition is fostered and the public is not deprived of the use of valuable, if not quite patentable, invention.[30]

In addition, by establishing legal remedies for trade secret misappropriation, trade secret law deters individuals who "have as their sole purpose and effect the redistribution of wealth from one firm to another."[31]

Historical Development of Trade Secret Law

Unlike other forms of intellectual property that can trace their origins back several hundreds of years, trade secret law is a creation of state court opinions from the middle of the 19th century. As noted by one legal scholar, the principles of trade secret law

> evolved out of a series of related common law torts: breach of confidence, breach of confidential relationship, common law misappropriation, unfair competition, unjust enrichment, and torts related to trespass or unauthorized access to a plaintiff's property. It

---

[29] ROGER E. SCHECHTER & JOHN R. THOMAS, INTELLECTUAL PROPERTY: THE LAW OF COPYRIGHTS, PATENTS AND TRADEMARKS, §24.

[30] *Kewanee Oil Co.*, 416 U.S. at 484-85.

[31] Rockwell Graphic Systems, Inc. v. DEV Industries, Inc., 925 F.2d 174, 178 (7th Cir. 1991).

also evolved out of a series of legal rules—contract and common law—governing the employment relationship.[32]

In 1939, the American Law Institute (ALI), a group of lawyers, judges, and legal scholars, published a treatise titled the "Restatement of Torts," which was an effort to provide a "clear formulation[]of common law and its statutory elements or variations and reflect the law as it presently stands or might plausibly be stated by a court."[33] The Restatement of Torts included two sections dealing with the law of trade secrets. Section 757 explained the subject matter of trade secrets, while Section 758 spelled out the elements of a trade secret misappropriation cause of action. The ALI later addressed trade secrets in sections 39-45 of its 1993 "Restatement (Third) of Unfair Competition."

In addition, the National Conference of Commissioners on Uniform State Law (NCCUSL) issued the Uniform Trade Secrets Act (UTSA) in 1979, which represents "the first comprehensive effort to codify the law of trade secrets protection, incorporating the major common law principles while filling gaps left by the courts."[34] The NCCUSL consists of a group of academics, attorneys, and judges who draft statutes addressing a variety of issues, and then propose that each state enact them.[35] However, the NCCUSL lacks direct legislative authority itself. Its uniform acts become law only to the extent that state legislatures choose to adopt them.

The federal government did not take steps to provide national trade secret protection until the mid-1990s, when Congress enacted the Economic Espionage Act of 1996. This federal criminal law is described in detail in the following section.

Current Legal Landscape for Trade Secret Protection

State Law

As noted in the section above, trade secrets primarily receive protection from misappropriation under state law. Individuals or corporations may seek civil damages in state courts by pursuing a common law tort action for misappropriation or through a specific state statute. The Uniform Trade Secrets Act (UTSA) codifies the basic principles of common law trade secret protection and has been adopted by 47 states and the District of Columbia,[36] although many state legislatures made some changes to the original model text before enacting it. These state laws provide definitions for the key terms "trade secret," "misappropriation," and "improper means,"[37] and specify various forms of injunctive and monetary relief (including compensatory damages,

---

[32] Mark A. Lemley, *The Surprising Virtues of Treating Trade Secrets as IP Rights,* 61 STANFORD L. REV. 311, 316 (2008).

[33] ALI, *Publications Catalog FAQ, at* http://www.ali.org/index.cfm?fuseaction=publications.faq.

[34] NCCUSL, *Why States Should Adopt UTSA, at* http://www.uniformlaws.org/Narrative.aspx?title= Why%20States%20Should%20Adopt%20UTSA.

[35] For more information about the NCCUSL, *see* http://www.uniformlaws.org/.

[36] Only New York, Massachusetts and North Carolina have not enacted the UTSA, though they offer protection through a distinct statute or the common law.

[37] Uniform Trade Secrets Act §1.

punitive damages, and attorney's fees) in a civil action for misappropriation of a trade secret.[38] A few states even recognize the theft of trade secrets as a prosecutable crime.[39]

Federal Law

Trade Secrets Act

Before 1996, arguably the most significant federal legislation regarding trade secrets was the Trade Secrets Act.[40] This statute, enacted in 1948, is actually of narrow applicability. It forbids federal government employees and government contractors from making an unauthorized disclosure of confidential government information, including trade secrets. The sanctions for violating this criminal offense are removal from office or employment, and a fine and/or imprisonment of not more than one year. The law does not apply to state or local government actors or to private sector employees.

Economic Espionage Act

In 1996, Congress enacted a far broader piece of legislation pertaining to trade secrets, the Economic Espionage Act of 1996 (EEA).[41] The legislative history of the EEA reveals the congressional concerns over growing international and domestic economic espionage against U.S. businesses that prompted the establishment of a more comprehensive, federal scheme protecting trade secrets:

> American companies and the U.S. Government spend billions on research and development. The benefits reaped from these expenditures can easily come to nothing, however, if a competitor can simply steal the trade secrets without expending the development costs. ... For years now, there has been mounting evidence that many foreign nations and their corporations have been seeking to gain competitive advantage by stealing the trade secrets, the intangible intellectual property of inventors in this country. ... [S]ince the end of the cold war, foreign nations have increasingly put their espionage resources to work trying to steal American economic secrets.[42]

The EEA defines two separate criminal offenses: (1) theft of a trade secret for the benefit of a foreign entity (economic espionage, 18 U.S.C. Section 1831), and (2) trade secret theft intended to confer an economic benefit to another party (theft of trade secrets, 18 U.S.C. Section 1832).[43] As a threshold matter, to trigger an action under either provision of the EEA, the information must qualify as a trade secret. The EEA expansively defines a "trade secret" to encompass

---

[38] Restatement (Third) of Unfair Competition §§44, 45 (1994).

[39] For example, California provides that anyone who acquires, discloses, or uses trade secrets without authorization shall be punished by imprisonment of up to one year in a county jail, by a fine of up to $5,000, or by both penalties. CAL. PENAL CODE §499c. In Texas, the knowing theft of a trade secret carries a criminal sentence of at least two years imprisonment (up to a maximum of 10 years) and a fine of up to $10,000. TEX. PENAL CODE §31.05. *See also* N.J. STAT. ANN. §2C:20-1; N.Y. PENAL LAW §165.07.

[40] 18 U.S.C. §1905.

[41] P.L. 104-294, 110 Stat. 3488 (1996).

[42] 142 CONG. REC. S12207, S12208 (daily ed. October 2, 1996) (statement of Sen. Specter).

[43] For a comprehensive description and analysis of all the statutory elements of the EEA, *see* CRS Report R42681, *Stealing Trade Secrets and Economic Espionage: An Overview of 18 U.S.C. 1831 and 1832*, by Charles Doyle.

[A]ll forms and types of financial, business, scientific, technical, economic, or engineering information, including patterns, plans, compilations, program devices, formulas, designs, prototypes, methods, techniques, processes, procedures, programs, or codes, whether tangible or intangible, and whether or how stored, compiled, or memorialized physically, electronically, graphically, photographically, or in writing if—

a) the owner thereof has taken reasonable measures to keep such information secret; and

b) the information derives independent economic value, actual or potential, from not being generally known to, and not being readily ascertainable through proper means by, the public.[44]

Economic Espionage

The EEA's "economic espionage" provision, 18 U.S.C. Section 1831, punishes those who misappropriate, or attempt or conspire to misappropriate, trade secrets with the intent or knowledge that the offense will benefit a foreign government, instrumentality, or agent.[45] Such misappropriation must have been committed "knowingly"; in other words, the individual must have known that the information taken was valuable to its owner and that its owner had taken steps to keep it confidential.[46]

According to the legislative history of the EEA, the "benefit" derived from a foreign espionage effort includes not only an economic benefit, but also "reputational, strategic, or tactical benefit."[47] A "foreign instrumentality" includes any "entity that is substantially owned, controlled, sponsored, commanded, managed, or dominated by a foreign government."[48] Therefore, a foreign corporation that engages in espionage without any evidence of sponsorship or control from a foreign government may not be subjected to a Section 1831 prosecution. However, an individual or organization that engages in theft of trade secrets, although not intending to benefit a foreign entity, could be liable for violating the more general criminal trade secrets provision contained in Section 1832, described in the section below.

Theft of Trade Secrets

The EEA's "theft of trade secrets" prohibition, 18 U.S.C. Section 1832, is of more general application. The principal elements of an EEA claim for theft of trade secrets are (1) the intentional and/or knowing theft, appropriation, destruction, alteration, or duplication of (2) a trade secret related to a product or service used in or intended for use in interstate or foreign

---

[44] 18 U.S.C. §1839(3). This definition is substantially similar to that used by the UTSA, although it is broader in coverage. For a comparison of the language of the EEA and UTSA, *see* James H.A. Pooley et al., *Understanding the Economic Espionage Act of 1996*, 5 TEX. INTELL. PROP. L.J. 177, 188-197 (1997).

[45] 18 U.S.C. §1831.

[46] The legislative history of the EEA opined that this mens rea element of the offense would not be too difficult for government prosecutors to establish: "Most companies go to considerable pains to protect their trade secrets. Documents are marked proprietary; security measures put in place; and employees often sign confidentiality agreements to ensure that the theft of intangible information is prohibited in the same way that the theft of physical items are protected." 142 CONG. REC. S12213 (daily ed. October 2, 1996) (Managers' Statement for H.R. 3723, The Economic Espionage Bill).

[47] H.R. Rep. No. 104-788, at 11 (1996).

[48] 18 U.S.C. §1839(1).

---

commerce (3) with intent to convert the trade secret and (4) intent or knowledge that such action will injure the owner.[49]

Scrutiny of these additional elements reveals several fundamental differences between Sections 1832 and 1831. First, Section 1832 does not require that the offense benefit or intend to benefit a foreign entity; it is a law of general applicability. Section 1832 also requires that the theft *economically* benefit someone other than the trade secret owner, whereas Section 1831, the foreign economic espionage provision, more broadly encompasses misappropriation for any purpose, including non-economic benefits such as "reputational, strategic, or tactical benefit[s]."[50] Establishing that the offender intended to cause injury to the trade secret owner "does not require the government to prove malice or evil intent, but merely that the actor knew or was aware to a practical certainty that his conduct would cause some disadvantage to the rightful owner."[51]

An FBI assistant director recently testified before Congress about the logistical difficulties of bringing a prosecution under Section 1831 compared to Section 1832:

> Often, the greatest challenge in prosecuting economic espionage, as opposed to trade secret theft, is being able to prove that the theft was intended to benefit a foreign government or foreign instrumentality. The beneficiary of the stolen trade secrets may be traced to an overseas entity, but obtaining evidence that proves the entity's relationship with a foreign government can be difficult. The decision to pursue these cases under Section 1832 (theft of trade secrets) instead of Section 1831 (economic espionage) may depend upon the availability of foreign evidence and witnesses, diplomatic concerns, and the presence of classified or sensitive information required to prove the foreign nexus element.[52]

Authorized Penalties Under the EEA

The EEA authorizes substantial criminal fines and imprisonment penalties for economic espionage and theft of trade secrets. For economic espionage, the maximum penalties increase to $5 million for individuals and imprisonment of 15 years;[53] in the case of corporations that are found guilty of this offense, the applicable maximum fine is the greater of (a) $10 million or (b) three times the value of the stolen trade secret.[54] Theft of trade secrets for commercial advantage is punishable by a fine of up to $250,000 for individuals as well as imprisonment of up to 10 years, whereas organizations can be fined up to $5 million.[55] The EEA also authorizes the criminal or civil forfeiture of "any property used, or intended to be used ... to commit or facilitate" an EEA violation as well as "any property constituting, or derived from, any proceeds

---

[49] 18 U.S.C. §1832.

[50] H.R. Rep. No. 104-788, at 11 (1996).

[51] *Id.* at 11-12.

[52] *Economic Espionage and Trade Secret Theft: Are Our Laws Adequate for Today's Threats?: Hearings Before the Senate Judiciary Comm., Subcomm. on Crime and Terrorism*, 113th Cong. 2d Sess. (2014) (statement of Randall C. Coleman, Assistant Director, Counterintelligence Division, FBI).

[53] 18 U.S.C. §1831.

[54] 18 U.S.C. §1831.

[55] 18 U.S.C. §1832.

obtained directly or indirectly as a result of" an EEA offense.[56] Offenders must also pay victims of trade secret theft restitution.[57]

In addition, during any prosecution or proceeding under the EEA, federal district courts are required to enter protective orders, or to take other measures, "as may be necessary and appropriate to preserve the confidentiality of trade secrets, consistent with the requirements of the Federal Rules of Criminal and Civil Procedure, the Federal Rules of Evidence, and all other applicable laws."[58] The legislative history of the EEA reveals the congressional interest in ensuring that courts use protective orders to guard against trade secret disclosures:

> We have been deeply concerned about the efforts taken by courts to protect the confidentiality of a trade secret. It is important that in the early stages of a prosecution the issue whether material is a trade secret not be litigated. Rather, courts should, when entering these orders, always assume that the material at issue is in fact a trade secret.[59]

The EEA also allows the Attorney General to bring a civil action to obtain "appropriate injunctive relief" against any violation of the EEA provisions regarding the protection of trade secrets.[60] However, the EEA does not provide victims of trade secret theft with a private civil cause of action.[61]

Extraterritorial Application of the EEA

Trade secret violations that occur both domestically and outside the United States may be subject to criminal prosecution by the federal government under the EEA. The U.S. Supreme Court has said on a number of occasions that "[i]t is a longstanding principle of American law 'that legislation of Congress, unless a contrary intent appears, is meant to apply only within the territorial jurisdiction of the United States'"[62] With this in mind, Congress specifically identified the circumstances under which it intended the economic espionage and theft of trade secrets provisions of the EEA to apply overseas.[63] Either offense may be prosecuted if (1) the offender is a U.S. citizen or permanent resident alien or an organization organized under U.S. law, or (2) an act in furtherance of the offense is committed within the United States.[64]

---

[56] 18 U.S.C. §§1834; 2323.

[57] *Id.*

[58] 18 U.S.C. §1835.

[59] 142 CONG. REC. S12213 (daily ed. October 2, 1996) (Managers' Statement for H.R. 3723, The Economic Espionage Bill).

[60] 18 U.S.C. §1836.

[61] *See* Barnes v. J.C. Penney Co., 2004 U.S. Dist. LEXIS 17557, *10 (N.D. Tex. 2004) (explaining that "[t]his criminal law provision [18 U.S.C. §1832] does not create a private cause of action. Any decision regarding prosecution under this provision is vested in the sole discretion of the United States Department of Justice and Plaintiff has no standing to seek relief under its terms.").

[62] *Morrison v. National Australia Bank Ltd.*, 130 S.Ct. 2869, 2877 (2010), quoting *EEOC v. Arabian American Oil Co.*, 499 U.S. 244, 248 (1991) and *Foley Bros., Inc. v. Filardo*, 336 U.S. 281 (1949). See generally, CRS Report 94-166, *Extraterritorial Application of American Criminal Law*, by Charles Doyle.

[63] H.Rept. 104-788, at 14 (1996).

[64] 18 U.S.C. §1837. This broad grant of extraterritorial authority may raise enforcement problems if an act of economic espionage does not have any connection with the United States. For example, it has been suggested that "if a United States citizen residing abroad steals a Russian trade secret on behalf of the Chinese government, that act is a violation of the EEA ... " James H.A. Pooley et al., *Understanding the Economic Espionage Act of 1996*, 5 TEX. INTELL. PROP. (continued...)

Statutory Exceptions to EEA Prohibitions

The EEA provides two express exceptions to the conduct that it prohibits (1) any otherwise lawful activity conducted by a governmental entity of the United States, a state, or a political subdivision of a state; or (2) the reporting of a suspected violation of law to any governmental entity of the United States, a state, or a political subdivision of a state, if such entity has lawful authority with respect to that violation.[65] The first exception permits the government to conduct an otherwise lawful "investigative, protective, or intelligence activity" with respect to the trade secret.[66] The second exception allows for the reporting of suspected criminal activity to law enforcement.[67]

Non-Preemption of Other Federal and State Laws

While the EEA was enacted in part due to the apparent shortcomings of other federal laws concerning the protection of trade secrets, the EEA expressly states that the act does not preempt or displace any other civil or criminal remedies provided by other federal or state laws for the misappropriation of a trade secret.[68] Federal prosecutors thus may bring criminal charges under the following laws in addition to, or instead of, the EEA, assuming that the conduct involved in the EEA violation also violates these federal criminal statutes: (1) the Computer Fraud and Abuse Act,[69] which penalizes anyone who accesses certain computers without authorization or in excess of authorization, with the intent to defraud; (2) the National Stolen Property Act (NSPA),[70] which prohibits the interstate transportation of tangible stolen "goods, wares, or merchandise," or the knowing receipt of such property; and (3) the federal wire fraud statute,[71] which makes it illegal to use wire, radio, or television communications for purposes of executing a scheme to defraud.

International Law

The United States offers a more sophisticated and robust legal regime protecting trade secrets than most other countries. It has been noted that,

---

(...continued)

L.J. 177, 204 (1997). Yet the Department of Justice would likely not bring an action under the EEA for this violation, "both to conserve its resources and to avoid the danger of intervening in what is essentially an internal dispute in a foreign country." *Id.*

[65] 18 U.S.C. §1833.

[66] H.R. Rep. No. 104-788, at 14 (1996).

[67] *Id.*

[68] 18 U.S.C. §1838.

[69] 18 U.S.C. §1030(a)(4), (e)(2). For more information about this statute, *see* CRS Report 97-1025, *Cybercrime: An Overview of the Federal Computer Fraud and Abuse Statute and Related Federal Criminal Laws*, by Charles Doyle.

[70] 18 U.S.C. §§2314, 2315. The NSPA has been interpreted by the federal courts to *exclude* the theft of *intangible* intellectual property. *See* United States v. Aleynikov, 676 F.3d 71, 77-78 (2d Cir. 2012) ("Some tangible property must be taken from the owner for there to be deemed a 'good' that is 'stolen' for purposes of the NSPA. ... [T]he theft and subsequent interstate transmission of purely intangible property is beyond the scope of the NSPA."); United States v. Agrawal, 726 F.3d 235, 252 (2d Cir. 2013) ("[A] defendant such as Agrawal, who steals papers on which intangible intellectual property is reproduced, does assume physical control over something tangible as is necessary for the item to be a 'good' ... for purposes of the NSPA.") (internal quotations and citations omitted).

[71] 18 U.S.C. §1343. For more information about this statute, *see* CRS Report R41930, *Mail and Wire Fraud: A Brief Overview of Federal Criminal Law*, by Charles Doyle.

Much of the rest of the world has very weak laws or enforcement practices, with the issue particularly acute in many of the largest emerging economies, such as China, Brazil, Russia, and India. Thus, as supply chains and operations expand globally, a company's ability to protect its trade secrets may be significantly diminished by weak rule of law and ineffective or non-existent enforcement in a number of countries.[72]

There is no international treaty specifically pertaining to the protection of trade secrets. However, one of the agreements reached during the Uruguay Round of Multilateral Trade Negotiations (that concluded with the signing of the Marrakesh Agreement Establishing the World Trade Organization (WTO))[73] was the Agreement on Trade-Related Aspects of Intellectual Property Rights (TRIPS). TRIPS establishes minimum standards of protection for patents, copyrights, trademarks, and trade secrets that each WTO signatory state must give to the intellectual property of fellow WTO members.[74] Compliance with TRIPS is a prerequisite for WTO membership.

TRIPS does not explicitly refer to "trade secrets." However, in order to "ensur[e] effective protection against unfair competition,"[75] TRIPS does refer to "protection of undisclosed information" and uses a definition that is similar to that of the traditional trade secret definition described above. Article 39 of TRIPS obliges WTO members to protect individuals and corporations[76] who own or control "undisclosed information" from unauthorized disclosure, acquisition, or use "without their consent in a manner contrary to honest commercial practices."[77] A footnote defines "a manner contrary to honest commercial practices" to mean "practices such as breach of contract, breach of confidence and inducement to breach, and includes the acquisition of undisclosed information by third parties who knew, or were grossly negligent in failing to know, that such practices were involved in the acquisition."[78]

Article 39 also defines "undisclosed information" as information that

1. "is secret in the sense that it is not, as a body or in the precise configuration and assembly of its components, generally known among or readily accessible to persons within the circles that normally deal with the kind of information in question;

2. has commercial value because it is secret; and

3. has been subject to reasonable steps under the circumstances, by the person lawfully in control of the information, to keep it secret."[79]

---

[72] George Washington University Homeland Security Policy Institute, *Economic Espionage and Trade Secret Theft: An Overview of the Legal Landscape and Policy Response,* at 5 (September 2013), *available at* http://homelandsecurity.gwu.edu/sites/homelandsecurity.gwu.edu/files/downloads/Covington_SpecialIssueBrief.pdf.

[73] For more information about the WTO, *see* CRS Report RS22154, *World Trade Organization (WTO) Decisions and Their Effect in U.S. Law,* by Jane M. Smith, Brandon J. Murrill, and Daniel T. Shedd.

[74] World Trade Organization, Understanding the WTO - Intellectual Property: Protection and Enforcement, *at* http://www.wto.org/english/thewto_e/whatis_e/tif_e/agrm7_e htm.

[75] TRIPS Agreement, art. 39, para. 1, *available at* http://www.wto.org/english/docs_e/legal_e/27-trips_04d_e htm#7.

[76] The TRIPS Agreement refers to "individuals and corporations" as "natural and legal persons."

[77] TRIPS Agreement, art. 39, para. 2.

[78] *Id.* n.10.

[79] *Id.,* art. 39, para. 2.

Note that unlike the federal Economic Espionage Act that provides an extensive list of the various types of information that may be considered a trade secret, Article 39 lacks such specificity and thus the term "information" could be subject to broad or narrow interpretation by WTO members. In addition, recent testimony before Congress criticized the vagueness of the protection mandated by Article 39:

> The heart of the relevant clause in TRIPS is vague; it asks whether the trade secret has been acquired or used "in a manner contrary to honest commercial practices." As a result, in Europe alone, trade secret law, which to date is not yet controlled by a European Union Directive, is a patchwork of different forms of protection. What is contrary to honest commercial practices in one country may be considered acceptable in other countries.[80]

Nevertheless, Article 39 of TRIPS is the first time that protection of trade secrets has appeared in a multilateral treaty.[81] According to a Suffolk University Law School professor, the "TRIPS Agreement includes a requirement that member nations enact trade secret law that is very similar to U.S. trade secret law. ... This is significant in light of the fact that trade secret law either did not exist or was undeveloped in many countries prior to the TRIPS Agreement."[82]

The WTO has the power to resolve disputes between member states for alleged violations of the TRIPS Agreement, including its provisions governing "undisclosed information." However, such cases appear to be very rare; a search of the WTO's dispute cases revealed that a complaint involving Article 39 has occurred only once, and that case was eventually withdrawn after the parties (China and the European Communities) reached an agreement in the form of a Memorandum of Understanding.[83] In May 2014, Senator Schumer sent a letter to the U.S. Trade Representative (USTR) Michael Froman, urging him to "initiate a case at the World Trade Organization (WTO) against China for state-backed cyber espionage against American businesses and workers."[84] The letter argues that Chinese policies that sanction cyber espionage are in clear violation of the TRIPS agreement that obliges WTO members to protect trade secrets.[85] As of the date of this report, the USTR has not filed a WTO complaint against China over this matter.[86]

The United States has entered into numerous bilateral and multilateral free trade agreements (FTAs) that require their signatories to provide higher levels of intellectual property protection than are required under the TRIPS Agreement. These intellectual property obligations exceed those of the TRIPS Agreement and are commonly referred to as "TRIPS-plus agreements." The United States has for many years pursued a policy of encouraging its trading partners to adopt TRIPS-plus provisions, which include more robust protections for trade secrets. Negotiating the inclusion of trade secret protection as part of these FTAs is discussed later in this report.

---

[80] *Trade Secrets: Promoting and Protecting American Innovation, Competitiveness and Market Access in Foreign Markets: Hearings Before the House Judiciary Comm., Subcomm. on Courts, Intellectual Property and Internet,* 113th Cong. 2d Sess. (2014) (statement of David M. Simon, Senior Vice President, salesforce.com, Inc.).

[81] Francois Dessemontet, *Arbitration and Confidentiality,* 7 AM. REV. INT'L ARB. 299, 307 (1996).

[82] Andrew Beckerman-Rodau, *Patent Law - Balancing Profit Maximization and Public Access to Technology,* 4 COLUM. SCI. & TECH. L. REV. 1, 20 n.108. (2002).

[83] WTO, Dispute Settlement DS372, *available at* http://www.wto.org/english/tratop_e/dispu_e/cases_e/ds372_e.htm.

[84] Senator Schumer, *Press Release: Schumer Calls on U.S. Trade Rep to File WTO Suit in Response to Chinese Cyber-Attacks,* May 22, 2014, *available at* http://www.schumer.senate.gov/Newsroom/record.cfm?id=351779.

[85] *Id.*

[86] For more information on this topic, *see* CRS Report IN10079, *Alleged Chinese Government Cyber Theft of U.S. Commercial Trade Secrets,* by Wayne M. Morrison, Susan V. Lawrence, and John W. Rollins.

The Growing Problem of Trade Secret Theft and Economic Espionage

Measuring Economic Loss

It is difficult to determine the total value of trade secrets to U.S. businesses, although a report issued by the U.S. Chamber of Commerce stated that "[p]ublicly traded U.S. companies own an estimated $5 trillion worth of trade secrets."[87] A recent study by PricewaterhouseCoopers (PwC) and the Center for Responsible Enterprise and Trade (CREATe.org) suggested that the economic loss attributable to trade secret theft is between 1% to 3% of U.S. Gross Domestic Product.[88] A more precise calculation of the economic impact of trade secret theft is impeded by several factors identified by the Office of the National Counterintelligence Executive (ONCIX):

1. A company may not realize that its sensitive information has been stolen until years after the crime.

2. Reporting security breaches to the FBI or other law enforcement entity could harm the company's reputation and stock prices, or damage its corporate relationships.

3. Publicly accusing a foreign government or business competitor of trade secret theft carries the risk of offending the company's potential customers or business partners.

4. It may be very difficult, if not impossible, to measure the monetary value of some forms of sensitive information.[89]

ONCIX further opined that the "[e]stimates from academic literature on the losses from economic espionage range so widely as to be meaningless—from $2 billion to $400 billion or more a year—reflecting the scarcity of data and the variety of methods used to calculate losses."[90]

Current Trends in Trade Secret Litigation

A law review article published in 2010 presented a statistical analysis of trade secret litigation in federal courts, in which it examined 394 federal court cases between 1950 and 2008 that related to trade secret law.[91] The study explained that it is difficult to provide a specific number of recent trade secret court cases in federal court because

---

[87] U.S. Chamber of Commerce, *The Case for Enhanced Protection of Trade Secrets in the Trans-Pacific Partnership Agreement,* at 10, *available at* https://www.uschamber.com/sites/default/files/legacy/international/files/Final%20TPP%20Trade%20Secrets%208_0.pdf.

[88] PwC & CREATe.org, *Economic Impact of Trade Secret Theft: A Framework for Companies to Safeguard Trade Secrets and Mitigate Potential Threats,* at 3 (February 2014), *available at* http://www.pwc.com/en_US/us/forensic-services/publications/assets/economic-impact.pdf.

[89] Office of the National Counterintelligence Executive, *Foreign Spies Stealing US Economic Secrets in Cyberspace,* October 2011, at 3.

[90] *Id.* at 4.

[91] David S. Almeling et al., *A Statistical Analysis of Trade Secret Litigation in Federal Courts,* 45 GONZAGA L. REV. (continued...)

the federal judiciary does not systematically track trade secret litigation. The Administrative Office of the U.S. Courts and the Federal Judicial Center collect information about federal litigation, and the resulting databases are widely used by legal researchers. The data include information about every case filed in federal courts, such as the subject matter of the case, the parties, and outcome. Although the databases include specific data for patent, copyright, and trademark cases, they include no specific data on trade secret cases, and it is nearly impossible to isolate trade secret cases from other civil cases based on their data.[92]

Nevertheless, the law review article concluded that, at the federal level, "trade secret litigation ... is growing exponentially," doubling from 1988 to 1995 and doubling again from 1995 to 2004.[93] The article projects that federal trade secret cases will double again by 2017.

The authors of that law review article also wrote an article that provided a statistical analysis of trade secret litigation in state courts, in which the authors examined 358 state appellate court decisions issued between 1995 and 2009.[94] The authors explained that only state appellate court opinions were considered because many state trial courts do not publish their decisions. The authors found that unlike the exponential growth of federal court trade secret cases, "state trade secret appellate decisions are increasing, but only in a linear pattern at a modest pace."[95] The authors noted that during the 15-year period of the study, "trade secret litigation in state courts had not doubled and, at the current rate of growth, is not expected to double for more than two decades."[96]

Types of Offenders

Domestic

In the vast majority (over 90%) of trade secret cases that are litigated in state court, the alleged misappropriator is someone the trade secret owner knows, either a current or former employee or a business partner.[97] Given this statistic, it has been suggested that "a prudent trade secret owner should focus its efforts in large part on protecting trade secrets from unscrupulous employees and, to a somewhat lesser extent, business partners."[98]

Foreign

In its October 2011 report to Congress, ONCIX warned that "[b]ecause the United States is a leader in the development of new technologies and a central player in global finance and trade networks, foreign attempts to collect US technological and economic information will continue at

---

(...continued)

291 (2010).

[92] *Id.* at 296.

[93] *Id.* at 293.

[94] David S. Almeling et al., *A Statistical Analysis of Trade Secret Litigation in State Courts*, 46 GONZAGA L. REV. 57 (2010).

[95] *Id.* at 61.

[96] *Id.* at 67.

[97] *Id.* at 68.

[98] *Id.*

a high level and will represent a growing and persistent threat to US economic security."[99] ONCIX raised particular concerns about the use of the Internet, computer technologies, and mobile communication devices to steal the trade secrets of U.S. businesses:

> [N]early all business records, research results, and other sensitive economic or technology-related information now exist primarily in digital form. Cyberspace makes it possible for foreign collectors to gather enormous quantities of information quickly and with little risk, whether via remote exploitation of victims' computer networks, downloads of data to external media devices, or e-mail messages transmitting sensitive information.[100]

While cyber-enabled methods of trade secret theft are getting increased attention from the federal government,[101] it is important to realize that many actors (foreign intelligence services, corporate competitors, transnational criminal organizations) "still rely on physical means such as recruitment of insiders and placement of agents within companies for purposes of stealing critical data."[102] The motivation for trade secret theft varies, with some perpetrators "seek[ing] personal financial gain, while others hope to advance national interests or political and social causes."[103]

According to ONCIX, the governments of China and Russia are particularly "aggressive and capable collectors of sensitive U.S. economic information and technologies," and "Chinese actors are the world's most active and persistent perpetrators of economic espionage."[104] The U.S. International Trade Commission (USITC) released a report indicating that U.S. firms lost approximately $1.1 billion in the year 2009 due to Chinese trade secret misappropriation.[105] Between January 2009 and January 2013, China was involved in 17 criminal prosecutions (out of a total of 20) that the U.S. Department of Justice brought pursuant to the EEA.[106]

Enforcement of Trade Secret Rights

Litigation and Prosecution

At the state level, enforcement of trade secret laws is generally the responsibility of the trade secret owner (by filing a civil suit in state court against an individual or organization alleged to

---

[99] Office of the National Counterintelligence Executive, *Foreign Spies Stealing US Economic Secrets in Cyberspace*, October 2011, at i, *available at* http://www.ncix.gov/publications/reports/fecie_all/Foreign_Economic_Collection_2011.pdf.

[100] *Id.* at iii.

[101] *See, e.g.*, CRS Report IN10079, *Alleged Chinese Government Cyber Theft of U.S. Commercial Trade Secrets*, by Wayne M. Morrison, Susan V. Lawrence, and John W. Rollins.

[102] PwC & CREATe.org, *Economic Impact of Trade Secret Theft: A Framework for Companies to Safeguard Trade Secrets and Mitigate Potential Threats*, at 4.

[103] *Id.* at 10.

[104] Office of the National Counterintelligence Executive, *Foreign Spies Stealing US Economic Secrets in Cyberspace*, October 2011, at i-ii.

[105] USITC, *China: Effects of Intellectual Property Infringement and Indigenous Innovation Policies on the U.S. Economy*, Investigation no. 332-519, USITC Publication 4226, May 2011, 3-42, *available at* http://www.usitc.gov/publications/332/pub4226.pdf.

[106] Executive Office of the President, *Administration Strategy on Mitigating the Theft of U.S. Trade Secrets*, February 2013, at 23-31, *available at* http://www.whitehouse.gov/sites/default/files/omb/IPEC/admin_strategy_on_mitigating_the_theft_of_u.s._trade_secrets.pdf.

have misappropriated the trade secret in order to obtain remedies such as injunctive relief and compensatory and punitive damages).[107] In addition, as discussed above, a few states have enacted criminal laws against trade secret theft under which state prosecutors may bring criminal charges against defendants in trade secret cases.

At the federal level, the Economic Espionage Unit located within the Federal Bureau of Investigation's (FBI's) Counterintelligence Division has primary responsibility for investigating offenses under the EEA.[108] The U.S. Department of Justice (DOJ) and its U.S. Attorneys have the power to prosecute cases involving corporate and state-sponsored trade secret theft.[109] The Attorney General is also authorized by the EEA to bring a civil action in federal court to obtain "appropriate injunctive relief" against any violation of the EEA.[110] However, as discussed in detail later in this report, federal law does not currently provide a private, federal cause of action for trade secret misappropriation.

Executive Branch Actions

Administration Strategy

In February 2013, the White House issued a report, *The Administration Strategy on Mitigating the Theft of U.S. Trade Secrets*, which describes its plan for "vigorously ... combat[ing] the theft of U.S. trade secrets that could be used by foreign companies or foreign governments to gain an unfair economic edge."[111] The report noted that the theft of valuable U.S. trade secrets has several negative consequences, including the loss of U.S. companies' intellectual property, the harm to American business innovation and global competitiveness, damage to national and economic security, possible reduction of U.S. exports, and the increased risk of American job losses.[112]

The report contains five "strategy action items" that are intended to provide a "means for improved coordination within the U.S. government" to protect the integrity of trade secrets:[113]

1. Focusing diplomatic efforts and pressure on other countries to protect trade secrets and discourage their theft, including (through the U.S. Trade Representative, or USTR) seeking provisions in bilateral, regional, and

---

[107] ROGER E. SCHECHTER & JOHN R. THOMAS, INTELLECTUAL PROPERTY: THE LAW OF COPYRIGHTS, PATENTS AND TRADEMARKS, §24.4.

[108] *Economic Espionage and Trade Secret Theft: Are Our Laws Adequate for Today's Threats?: Hearings Before the Senate Judiciary Comm., Subcomm. on Crime and Terrorism*, 113th Cong. 2d Sess. (2014) (statement of Randall C. Coleman, Assistant Director, Counterintelligence Division, FBI).

[109] The 93 U.S. Attorneys' Offices located across the United States and its territories have primary responsibility for prosecution of intellectual property offenses. Every office has at least one Computer Hacking and Intellectual Property (CHIP) Coordinator, who are Assistant U.S. Attorneys with expertise in prosecuting IP and computer crimes. U.S. Dep't of Justice, Computer Crime & Intellectual Property Section, Prosecuting Intellectual Property Crimes (4th ed. 2013), *available at* http://www.justice.gov/criminal/cybercrime/docs/prosecuting_ip_crimes_manual_2013.pdf.

[110] 18 U.S.C. §1836.

[111] Executive Office of the President, *Administration Strategy on Mitigating the Theft of U.S. Trade Secrets*, February 2013, at 1-2.

[112] *Id.* at 1.

[113] *Id.* at 2.

multilateral trade agreements[114] that require parties to establish remedies for trade secret theft similar to those provided for in U.S. law;

2. Promoting the development and adoption of voluntary best practices by private industry to protect trade secrets;

3. Enhancing domestic law enforcement operations by having the FBI and DOJ prioritize trade secret theft investigations and prosecutions, as well as having the Office of the Director of National Intelligence share information with the private sector about potential foreign espionage threats;

4. Improving domestic legislation to ensure that federal laws are effective in protecting trade secrets; and

5. Conducting education and outreach efforts to raise public awareness of the detrimental effects of trade secret theft.

Special 301

The USTR is required[115] to conduct an annual review of foreign countries' intellectual property policies and practices and to publish a "Special 301" Report that identifies countries that lack adequate and effective intellectual property protection and enforcement regimes. The 2013 Special 301 Report was the first time that the USTR included a section dedicated to "the growing problem of misappropriation of trade secrets in China and elsewhere."[116] The Report "urge[d] its trading partners to ensure that they have robust systems for protecting trade secrets, including deterrent penalties for criminal trade secret theft" and promised that the "USTR will monitor developments in this area."[117]

In a recent congressional hearing, a witness described the negative consequences of overseas trade secret theft as follows: "Inadequate protection of trade secrets abroad harms not only companies whose property is stolen, but also the country where the theft occurs, because companies are then less likely to form joint ventures and make high-value global supply chain investments in those countries."[118]

Free Trade Agreements (TPP and TTIP)

Currently, the USTR is seeking to improve trade secret protection in countries with which it is negotiating two free trade agreements: (1) the Trans-Pacific Partnership (TPP),[119] which involves

---

[114] For a comprehensive explanation of how the federal government may promote the protection of U.S. intellectual property through its international trade policy, *see* CRS Report RL34292, *Intellectual Property Rights and International Trade*, by Shayerah Ilias Akhtar and Ian F. Fergusson.

[115] P.L. 93-618, as amended by P.L. 100-418.

[116] USTR, *2013 Special 301 Report*, at 4 (May 2013), *available at* http://www.ustr.gov/sites/default/files/05012013%202013%20Special%20301%20Report.pdf.

[117] *Id.* at 13.

[118] *Trade Secrets: Promoting and Protecting American Innovation, Competitiveness and Market Access in Foreign Markets: Hearings Before the House Judiciary Comm., Subcomm. on Courts, Intellectual Property and Internet*, 113th Cong. 2d Sess. (2014) (statement of Thaddeus Burns, Senior Counsel, General Electric, on behalf of the Intellectual Property Owners Association).

[119] For more information on the TPP and intellectual property rights, *see* CRS Report R42694, *The Trans-Pacific Partnership (TPP) Negotiations and Issues for Congress*, coordinated by Ian F. Fergusson.

---

11 countries in the Asia-Pacific region, and (2) the Transatlantic Trade and Investment Partnership (TTIP),[120] with the European Union. The U.S. Chamber of Commerce has argued that the legal regimes of TPP countries need significant improvement in the area of trade secret protection:

> Some TPP countries, such as Canada, Australia, Malaysia, and Singapore, have no laws criminalizing traditional trade secret disclosure or misappropriation. ... Among those countries that do criminalize trade secret misappropriation or disclosure, the penalties often vary from those that would not provide sufficient deterrent effect to those that would but only if applied consistently. ... The low criminal penalties or lack thereof in some TPP jurisdictions are particularly troublesome, as criminal penalties are believed to provide a greater deterrent to the would-be trade secret thief than the prospect of a civil penalty alone.[121]

Such variation in trade secret protection is also present in the TTIP negotiations, as the European Union currently lacks a consistent, harmonized legal system governing trade secret protection; instead, there are disparities across the 27 EU Member States in "what [trade secrets] can be protected, in what circumstances, and what the courts can or will do."[122]

Limitations of Current Law and Proposed Changes

It has been argued that "federal law has not kept pace with the technological innovation that has enabled increased trade secret theft."[123] The lack of a federal civil cause of action for trade secret misappropriation is perhaps the most widely cited deficiency in U.S. trade secret law. As one legal practitioner has argued,

> Unfortunately the EEA has not deterred trade secret theft and foreign economic espionage. The Computer Crime and Intellectual Property Section of the United States Department of Justice has done an excellent job, but the burden on the government is too great. Without a federal civil cause of action, U.S. companies cannot adequately protect U.S. trade secret assets in a worldwide economy that now crosses international boundaries.[124]

Another problem companies have encountered in having only federal criminal statutes protecting trade secrets is that "criminal law punishes the defendant, but the process for compensating the victim is unwieldy, particularly when compared to relief available under civil law."[125] Others have

---

[120] For more information on the TTIP and intellectual property rights, *see* CRS Report R43387, *Transatlantic Trade and Investment Partnership (TTIP) Negotiations*, by Shayerah Ilias Akhtar and Vivian C. Jones.

[121] U.S. Chamber of Commerce, *The Case for Enhanced Protection of Trade Secrets in the Trans-Pacific Partnership Agreement*, at 23.

[122] Robert Anderson & Sarah Turner, *Report on Trade Secrets for the European Commission* (January 2012), at 44, *available at* http://ec.europa.eu/internal_market/iprenforcement/docs/trade-secrets/120113_study_en.pdf.

[123] *Trade Secrets: Promoting and Protecting American Innovation, Competitiveness and Market Access in Foreign Markets: Hearings Before the House Judiciary Comm., Subcomm. on Courts, Intellectual Property and Internet*, 113th Cong. 2d Sess. (2014) (statement of Thaddeus Burns, Senior Counsel, General Electric, on behalf of the Intellectual Property Owners Association).

[124] R. Mark Halligan, *Protecting U.S. Trade Secret Assets in the 21st Century*, 6:1 LANDSLIDE (September/October 2013), *available at* http://www.americanbar.org/publications/landslide/2013-14/september-october-2013/protecting_us_trade_secret_assets_the_21st_century.html.

[125] *Economic Espionage and Trade Secret Theft: Are Our Laws Adequate for Today's Threats?: Hearings Before the* (continued...)

---

highlighted the limitations of the EEA's extraterritorial application, noting that "prosecutors lack enforcement and proper service mechanisms against individuals and entities located outside the United States ... Prosecutors cannot charge alleged violators of the EEA until they cross U.S. borders."[126] Reportedly, since the enactment of the EEA in 1996, there have been relatively few cases prosecuted under the law: approximately 125 indictments[127] and 10 convictions.[128]

In Support of a Federal Civil Cause of Action for Trade Secret Theft

Some observers have urged Congress to adopt a comprehensive, federal trade secret law in order to promote uniformity in trade secret law throughout the United States.[129] Supporters of such legislation have argued that a federal trade secrets law would create procedural and substantive standards for the trade secret misappropriation offense on a uniform nationwide basis, in response to the current situation of state trade secret laws in which there are "fundamental differences about what constitutes a trade secret, what is required to misappropriate it, and what remedies are available" due to state-by-state variations in statutory text and state court interpretations.[130] In addition, Senator Coons has observed that, in contrast to state courts, "[f]ederal courts are better suited to working across state and national boundaries to facilitate discovery, serve defendants or witnesses, or prevent a party from leaving the country."[131] Representative Nadler has also asserted that the limitations of state trade secret law are impediments to the effective protection of U.S. corporate trade secrets in a global economy:

> While this system [of state law remedies] appears to have worked relatively well for local and intrastate disputes, it has not proven efficient or effective for [trade secret theft] incidents that cross state, and sometimes international, borders. ...
>
> [A] fifty-state system does not work well in our increasingly mobile and globally interconnected world. Former employees and industrial spies are likely to carry or transfer secret information across state borders or overseas. The limited jurisdiction of the state court system makes it more difficult to obtain discovery or to act quickly enough to enforce an order that might stop the immediate loss of company secrets.[132]

(...continued)

Senate Judiciary Comm., Subcomm. on Crime and Terrorism, 113th Cong. 2d Sess. (2014) (statement of Douglas K. Norman, Vice President & General Patent Counsel, Eli Lilly and Company).

[126] *The Report of the Commission on the Theft of American Intellectual Property,* at 42 (May 2013).

[127] *Can You Keep a Secret?,* THE ECONOMIST, March 16, 2013.

[128] *Economic Espionage and Trade Secret Theft: Are Our Laws Adequate for Today's Threats?: Hearings Before the Senate Judiciary Comm., Subcomm. on Crime and Terrorism*, 113th Cong. 2d Sess. (2014) (statement of Randall C. Coleman, Assistant Director, Counterintelligence Division, FBI); *see also* News Release, *Senator Coons, Hatch Introduce Bill to Combat Theft of Trade Secrets and Protect Jobs,* April 29, 2014, *at* http://www.coons.senate.gov/ newsroom/releases/release/senators-coons-hatch-introduce-bill-to-combat-theft-of-trade-secrets-and-protect-jobs ("Current federal criminal law is insufficient. Although the Economic Espionage Act of 1996 made trade secret theft a crime, the Department of Justice brought only 25 trade secret theft cases last year.").

[129] *See, e.g.,* Marina Lao, *Federalizing Trade Secrets Law in an Information Economy,* 59 OHIO STATE L. J. 1633 (1998); Rebel J. Pace, *The Case for a Federal Trade Secrets Act,* 8 HARVARD J. OF LAW & TECHNOLOGY (1995).

[130] David S. Almeling, *Four Reasons to Enact a Federal Trade Secrets Act,* FORDHAM INTELLECTUAL PROPERTY, MEDIA & ENTERTAINMENT LAW JOURNAL XIX.3 (2009), at 774.

[131] News Release, *Senators Coons, Hatch Introduce Bill to Combat Theft of Trade Secrets and Protect Jobs,* April 29, 2014.

[132] Press Release, *Rep. Nadler on Protecting Trade Secrets of American Companies,* June 24, 2014, *available at* (continued...)

Some commentators argue that trade secrets deserve to receive the same robust legal protections available to the three other types of intellectual property.[133] For example, owners of patents, copyright, and trademarks have the right to file a lawsuit against infringers in federal court to recover damages and possibly to enjoin further infringement, and yet there is no similar right afforded to trade secret owners,[134] despite the fact that trade secrets are often considered by many companies as their most valuable and important intellectual property asset.[135] Instead, at the federal level, companies must rely on the federal government (and its limited resources) to enforce their trade secret rights.

Supporters of a federal civil remedy for trade secret misappropriation believe that Congress should empower federal courts to issue ex parte orders to seize stolen trade secrets in certain limited circumstances, such as "to prevent an imminent misappropriation, the dissemination of a stolen trade secret, and to preserve evidence."[136] However, they note that any legislation should contain proper safeguards to prevent abuse of the ex parte process, "including damages in the event of wrongful seizure and protection of the information seized to protect against inappropriate access to the information."[137]

Finally, it has been asserted that "the United States has not consistently received cooperation from international jurisdictions in protecting trade secrets in part because it does not have its own federal civil statute to reference in encouraging the adoption and enforcement of similar legislation by its treaty partners."[138]

In Opposition to a Federal Civil Trade Secret Remedy

The establishment of a federal civil trade secret remedy has many proponents, yet there have been some opposing views. In 2007, the Trade Secrets Committee of the American Intellectual

---

(...continued)

http://nadler house.gov/press-release/rep-nadler-protecting-trade-secrets-american-companies.

[133] *Id.* (noting that U.S. law "already protect[s] trademarks, copyrights, and patents through federal civil remedies. It is time to do the same for trade secrets."); *Economic Espionage and Trade Secret Theft: Are Our Laws Adequate for Today's Threats?: Hearings Before the Senate Judiciary Comm., Subcomm. on Crime and Terrorism*, 113th Cong. 2d Sess. (2014) (statement of Drew Greenblatt, President and Owner, Marlin Steel Wire Products) ("Despite their strategic economic importance, trade secrets misappropriation is the only form of U.S. intellectual property violation for which the owner lacks access to federal court. This leaves U.S. firms without a key tool to prevent trade secret theft and recover any losses.").

[134] *Trade Secrets: Promoting and Protecting American Innovation, Competitiveness and Market Access in Foreign Markets: Hearings Before the House Judiciary Comm., Subcomm. on Courts, Intellectual Property and Internet*, 113th Cong. 2d Sess. (2014) (statement of Thaddeus Burns, Senior Counsel, General Electric, on behalf of the Intellectual Property Owners Association).

[135] U.S. Chamber of Commerce, *The Case for Enhanced Protection of Trade Secrets in the Trans-Pacific Partnership Agreement*, at 10; *see also* David Kappos, *Trade Secrets: Promise of Federal Protection Brings New Hope for Critical IP Law*, TheHill.com, June 30, 2014, *at* http://thehill.com/blogs/congress-blog/technology/210848-trade-secrets-promise-of-federal-protection-brings-new-hope ("Despite accounting for an average of two-thirds of U.S. companies' information value, trade secrets suffer from extremely limited recognition under federal law.").

[136] *Trade Secrets: Promoting and Protecting American Innovation, Competitiveness and Market Access in Foreign Markets: Hearings Before the House Judiciary Comm., Subcomm. on Courts, Intellectual Property and Internet*, 113th Cong. 2d Sess. (2014) (statement of Thaddeus Burns, Senior Counsel, General Electric, on behalf of the Intellectual Property Owners Association).

[137] *Id.*

[138] *Id.*

Property Law Association (AIPLA) issued a report that advised against federalizing trade secret law, in part out of a concern that such action may create additional burdens and costs upon the federal judiciary:

> The Committee believes that the problem of disparate state trade secret laws may have been overstated, because the various state statutes share much in common, especially those based upon the Uniform Trade Secrets Act (UTSA). Furthermore, many trade secret cases are already heard in federal court through diversity or supplemental jurisdiction, providing at least federal procedure, if not substantive law, benefits to private litigants. Others have argued, and the Committee agrees, that the current state regulation of trade secrets, although far from perfect, is functioning adequately and that federalizing state trade secret law would, therefore, needlessly burden the already overworked federal judiciary.[139]

However, AIPLA has since changed its position on this matter, as revealed in an April 2013 letter to the U.S. Intellectual Property Enforcement Coordinator (IPEC). In response to the IPEC's request for public comments for an administration legislative review related to economic espionage and trade secret theft, the President of AIPLA wrote that because of the increase in foreign trade secret theft in recent years, "AIPLA believes that the time has come to consider a federal civil remedy for international trade secret misappropriation."[140] Furthermore, the AIPLA letter argued that "[a]ny federal legislation should not preempt state trade secret laws, but should instead complement them and should provide jurisdiction for civil actions involving claims involving the international theft of trade secrets."[141]

Two law school professors have urged Congress to reject several pieces of pending trade secret legislation (specifically, the Defend Trade Secrets Act of 2014 (DTSA) and the Trade Secrets Protection Act of 2014 (TSPA), which are discussed in detail in the following section of this report) because they believe that the bills "will create or exacerbate many existing legal problems but solve none."[142] The letter, dated August 26, 2014, was signed by 31 professors who teach intellectual property law, trade secret law, innovation policy, and information law throughout the United States. In the view of the law professors who wrote or signed the letter, the DTSA and TSPA, which would establish a new private cause of action under the EEA, are not necessary and could even cause unintentional harm, for the following five reasons:[143]

1. Effective and uniform state law already exists.

2. The legislation will damage trade secret law and jurisprudence by weakening uniformity while simultaneously creating parallel, redundant and/or damaging law.

3. The legislation could be used for anti-competitive purposes.

---

[139] American Intellectual Property Law Association, *Report of the AIPLA Trade Secrets Committee* (2007), at 2, *available at* http://www2.aipla.org/MSTemplate.cfm?Section=Proposal_to_Federalize_Trade_Secret_Law&Site=Trade_Secret_Law&Template=/ContentManagement/ContentDisplay.cfm&ContentID=7041.

[140] AIPLA Comments on Trade Secret Theft Strategy Legislative Review, April 22, 2013, at 2, *available at* http://www.aipla.org/advocacy/executive/Documents/AIPLA%20Letter%20to%20IPEC%20on%20Trade%20Secrets%20-%204.22.13.pdf.

[141] *Id.* at 3.

[142] Professors' Letter in Opposition to the "Defend Trade Secrets Act of 2014" (S. 2267) and the "Trade Secrets Protection Act of 2014" (H.R. 5233), August 26, 2014, *available at* http://cyberlaw.stanford.edu/files/blogs/FINAL%20Professors%27%20Letter%20Opposing%20Trade%20Secret%20Legislation.pdf.

[143] *Id.* at 2-5.

4. The legislation increases the risk of accidental disclosure of trade secrets.

5. The legislation could have ancillary negative impacts on information access, business collaboration, and labor mobility.

The law professors' letter concludes by asserting that

> The Acts are incomplete solutions because the definition of a trade secret under US (and international law) is limited and does not protect all of the information that may be the subject of cyber-espionage, or even all of the information that many businesses believe are trade secrets. The Acts are ill-advised because they focus on trade secret misappropriation instead of the bad acts of cyber-espionage and foreign espionage–*which is where Congress should focus its legislative efforts*. Finally, the Acts are dangerous because the many downsides explained above have no—not one—corresponding upside.[144]

An attorney who specializes in patent and trade secret litigation has identified two potential problems with federal legislation, such as the DTSA,[145] that does not expressly preempt state trade secret laws:

> First, the need for the DTSA stems in part from state-by-state variations in trade secret laws and the transactional and substantive problems that such variations impose. The DTSA leaves those variations in place. Worse, the DTSA adds another law to the already cluttered landscape of 48 UTSA states (with their variations), two non-UTSA states, the federal Economic Espionage Act, and a federal common trade secret law.

> Second, the DTSA opens a backdoor to common-law and other causes of action that are precluded in most states. The UTSA "displaces tort, restitutionary, and other laws...providing civil remedies for misappropriation of a trade secret." The DTSA doesn't displace anything.

> Under the DTSA, trade secret plaintiffs would have the option of pursuing their claim in state or federal court and, if they choose federal court, the additional option of asserting duplicative causes of actions that aren't available in state courts.[146]

Legislation in the 113th Congress

The following section summarizes the key provisions of legislative proposals that have been introduced in the 113th Congress related to trade secret misappropriation.

S. 884, Deter Cyber Theft Act

Introduced by Senator Carl Levin, the Deter Cyber Theft Act would require the Director of National Intelligence (DNI) to submit an annual report to Congress that identifies foreign countries that engage in economic or industrial espionage in cyberspace with respect to U.S. trade

---

[144] *Id.* at 6-7 (emphasis in original, citation omitted).

[145] The DTSA has a "rule of construction" provision that expresses that Congress does not intend for the DTSA "to preempt any other provision of law." S. 2267, §2(e).

[146] David S. Almeling, *Guest Post: Defend Trade Secrets Act – A Primer, an Endorsement, and a Criticism*, Patently-O, May 30, 2014, *at* http://patentlyo.com/patent/2014/05/secrets-endorsement-criticism.html.

secrets.[147] Countries that the DNI determines to have conducted the most egregious forms of such espionage are to be placed on a priority watch list. The report must also identify (1) technologies or proprietary information developed by U.S. businesses that have been the target of cyber theft, (2) goods and services made or provided using such technologies or proprietary information, and (3) foreign entities, including those owned or controlled by foreign governments, that engage in, support, facilitate, or benefit from the cyber theft of U.S. trade secrets. The legislation would then require the President to direct the U.S. Customs and Border Protection to exclude from entry into the United States any goods produced or exported by the foreign entities identified in the report, if the President has determined that such exclusion is necessary to enforce intellectual property rights or to protect the integrity of the Department of Defense supply chain.[148]

H.R. 2281 / S. 1111, Cyber Economic Espionage Accountability Act

Introduced in the House by Representative Mike Rogers and in the Senate by Senator Ron Johnson, the Cyber Economic Espionage Accountability Act would require the President to submit to Congress a list of foreign government officials or persons acting on behalf of a foreign government that the President determines, based on credible information, are responsible for cyber espionage of intellectual property of U.S. persons or have acted as an agent of, or on behalf of, a person in a matter relating to such cyber espionage activity.[149] The President would be required to update this list as necessary and make the list publicly available in unclassified form, although individuals may be listed in a classified annex if the President determines that it is vital for U.S. national security interests to do so.[150] The act would render any aliens appearing on this list ineligible to receive a visa to enter the United States or be admitted to the United States[151] and would require the Secretary of State to revoke an alien's current visa or other documentation if an alien is on the list.[152] However, the Secretary would be given the power to waive such ineligibility or revocation in order to comply with international obligations or for national security purposes.[153] The act also contains several financial measures, including a provision that would require the President to

> exercise all powers granted by the International Emergency Economic Powers Act ... to the extent necessary to freeze and prohibit all transactions in all property and interests in property of a person who is on the list ... if such property and interests are in the United States, come within the United States, or are or come within the possession or control of a United States person.[154]

Another financial provision would require the Secretary of the Treasury to include anyone who is "on the list of specially designated nationals and blocked persons maintained by the Office of Foreign Assets Control of the Department of the Treasury."[155]

---

[147] S. 884, §2(a).

[148] *Id.* §2 (b).

[149] H.R. 2281, S. 1111, §3(a).

[150] *Id.* §3(b), (c).

[151] *Id.* §4(a).

[152] *Id.* §4(b).

[153] *Id.* §4(c).

[154] *Id.* §5(a).

[155] *Id.* §5(c).

S. 1770, the Future of American Innovation and Research (FAIR) Act of 2013

Introduced by Senator Flake, the Future of American Innovation and Research (FAIR) Act would create federal civil liability for trade secret misappropriation in certain circumstances: extraterritorial misappropriation or misappropriation of U.S. trade secrets for the benefit of foreign entities. If enacted, the legislation would provide the owner of a "covered trade secret" with the right to bring a civil action in federal court against a person who misappropriates, threatens to misappropriate, or conspires to misappropriate, the trade secret, if that person either (1) is located abroad, or (2) is acting on behalf of, or for the benefit of, a foreign person.[156] In addition, the FAIR Act would apply to extraterritorial conduct if such foreign conduct, "either by itself or in combination with conduct within the territorial jurisdiction of the United States, causes or is reasonably anticipated to cause an injury" (1) within the United States or (2) to a U.S. person.[157]

In establishing this private cause of action, the bill includes several relevant definitions, including

- "Covered trade secret": a trade secret that is related to or included in a product or service that is used or reasonably anticipated to be used in interstate or foreign commerce.

- "Improper means": includes theft, bribery, misrepresentation, breach of a duty to maintain secrecy, and espionage through electronic or other means.

- "Misappropriate": (1) acquire a trade secret of another by improper means, if the person who acquires it knows or has reason to know that the acquisition is by improper means, or (2) disclose or use a trade secret without express or implied consent by a person who used improper means to acquire knowledge of the trade secret or, at the time of disclosure or use, the person knew or had reason to know that the trade secret was obtained through improper means or acquired under circumstances giving rise to a duty to maintain its secrecy.

- "Person": includes a natural person, corporation, estate, government, or any other legal or commercial entity.

- "Trade secret": any information, including a formula, pattern, compilation, program, device, method, technique, or process, that (1) derives independent economic value from not being generally known to the public, and (2) is the subject of reasonable efforts to maintain the secrecy of the information.[158]

The FAIR Act would authorize a court to issue the following types of remedies in this civil action:

1. An order for appropriate injunctive relief against the offending conduct.

2. An order requiring affirmative actions to be taken to protect a covered trade secret from further misappropriation.

---

[156] S. 1770, §3(a).

[157] *Id.* §3(c).

[158] *Id.* §2.

3. An order requiring payment of a reasonable royalty for any ongoing disclosure or use of a covered secret (in a situation where the court finds that it would be unreasonable to prohibit further possession, disclosure, or use of the trade secret).

4. An award of damages for the actual loss caused by the misappropriation.

5. An award of damages for any unjust enrichment caused by the misappropriation that is not addressed in computing the damages for actual loss.

6. An award of punitive or exemplary damages (up to 2 times the award of damages in the two lines above) if the court finds that the trade secret was willfully or maliciously misappropriated.

7. An award of reasonable costs and attorney's fees to the prevailing party in the following three circumstances: (1) if a claim of misappropriation is made in bad faith, (2) if a motion to terminate an injunction is made or opposed in bad faith, and (3) if a trade secret is willfully or maliciously misappropriated.[159]

The FAIR Act includes an affirmative defense to the civil action if each alleged trade secret in the dispute was "readily ascertainable through proper means by other persons who did not already know the trade secret at the time of any alleged misappropriation, threat to misappropriate, or conspiracy to misappropriate."[160] The bill would establish a three-year statute of limitations for this civil action; that is, a civil action cannot be initiated later than three years after the date on which the offending conduct "that forms the basis for the action was discovered or by the exercise of reasonable diligence should have been discovered."[161]

Finally, the FAIR Act would grant a court discretionary power, upon ex parte application, to issue an order that provides for the preservation of evidence in the civil action and the seizure of any property (including computers) used, in any manner or part, to commit or facilitate the commission of the misappropriation that is alleged in the civil action.[162] The seizure order would be carried out by a federal law enforcement officer (such as a U.S. marshal) and the seized items would be taken into the custody of the court.[163] This seizure order may only be issued if

1. the applicant provides a bond in an amount that the court determines is adequate to pay any damages for a wrongful seizure;

2. the court finds that specific facts clearly show that (A) an ex parte seizure order is the only adequate means of effectively causing the end of the offending conduct; (B) the applicant has not publicized the requested seizure; (C) the applicant is likely to succeed on the merits of the case; (D) the applicant will suffer an immediate and irreparable injury if the seizure is not ordered; (E) the matter to be seized is located at the place identified in the application; (F) the harm to the applicant that would be caused by denying the seizure order outweighs the harm to the legitimate interests of the person against whom seizure is sought that would be caused by issuing the seizure order; and (G) if the person

---

[159] *Id.* §4.

[160] *Id.* §5(a)(2).

[161] *Id.* §5(e).

[162] *Id.* §6(a). The ex parte seizure order provision that appears in the FAIR Act appears to be modeled on existing procedures for seizing goods and counterfeit trademarks under the Trademark Act (15 U.S.C. §116(d)).

[163] S. 1770, §6(c).

whom seizure is sought would destroy, move, or hide the matter to be seized if the applicant were to notify that person in advance of such seizure.[164]

The FAIR Act would require the court to set a hearing date, between 3 days and 10 days after the seizure order is issued, for the court to determine whether the seized items should remain in the custody of the court. At the seizure hearing, the party that applied for the seizure order would have the burden of proving that the factual and legal grounds necessary to support the seizure order are still in effect; if that party fails to meet this burden, the court would be required to dissolve or modify the seizure order.[165]

The FAIR Act would authorize another cause of action available to a party that is injured by the seizure and that prevails in the civil action.[166] That party would be allowed to bring a civil action against the applicant for the seizure order to recover reasonable costs and attorney's fees incurred in the defense against the seizure order, and lost profits and punitive damages if the seizure order was sought in bad faith.

H.R. 2466, Private Right of Action Against Theft of Trade Secrets Act of 2013

The Private Right of Action Against Theft of Trade Secrets Act of 2013, introduced by Representative Lofgren, would amend the Economic Espionage Act of 1996 to authorize any person who suffers injury due to a violation of the EEA's "theft of trade secrets" prohibition, 18 U.S.C. Section 1832, to file a federal civil action against the violator, in order to obtain "appropriate compensatory damages and injunctive relief or other equitable relief."[167] The act would also establish a "negative" definition of the phrase "without authorization," as the language is used in in Section 1832, to *exclude* "independent derivation or working backwards from a lawfully obtained known product or service to divine the process which aided its development or manufacture." Thus, a person who discerns the subject matter of a trade secret through independent discovery or reverse-engineering would not be considered to have violated the "without authorization" element of Section 1832.[168] Note that this legislation would not amend 18 U.S.C. Section 1831, the EEA's "economic espionage" provision; thus, under this act, a victim of foreign economic espionage would not be given a right to file a civil action for a violation of Section 1831.

S. 2384, Deter Cyber Theft Act of 2014

Introduced by Senator Carl Levin on May 22, 2014, S. 2384, Deter Cyber Theft Act of 2014, is a new version of S. 884, Deter Cyber Theft Act, that he had sponsored in the first session of the 113th Congress. Senator Levin explained that the revised legislation was in response "to overwhelming and indisputable evidence of large scale cyber intrusions by the Government of China into the computer networks of private U.S. companies for the purpose of stealing valuable

---

[164] *Id.* §6(b).

[165] *Id.* §6(e).

[166] *Id.* §6(f).

[167] H.R. 2466, §2, adding a new subsection (c) to 18 U.S.C. §1832.

[168] *Id.* §2, adding a new subsection (d) to 18 U.S.C. §1832.

intellectual property and proprietary information."[169] One difference between S. 884 and S. 2384 is that the new version of the act would require the President, rather than the Director of National Intelligence, to annually submit to Congress the watch list of foreign countries that engage in economic or industrial espionage in cyberspace with respect to U.S. trade secrets or proprietary information.[170] Another difference is that S. 884 would require the President to direct the U.S. Customs and Border Protection to block the importation of certain articles that are produced or exported by the foreign entities named on the watch list, whereas S. 2384 would instead authorize the President, pursuant to the International Emergency Economic Powers Act, to block and prohibit all transactions in property, and interests in property, of foreign persons that the "President determines knowingly requests, engages in, supports, facilitates, or benefits from the significant appropriation, through economic or industrial espionage in cyberspace, of technologies or proprietary information developed by United States persons," if such property and interests in property are (1) in the United States; (2) come within the United States; or (3) are, or come within, the possession or control of a U.S. person.[171] (This sanction is similar to that proposed in S. 1111, the Cyber Economic Espionage Accountability Act, described above.)

S. 2267, the Defend Trade Secrets Act of 2014

Senator Coons introduced the Defend Trade Secrets Act of 2014 (DTSA) on April 29, 2014. He argued that the legislation would "finally give trade secrets the same legal protections that other forms of critical intellectual property already enjoy" (in terms of allowing the rights holder to bring lawsuits in federal court against those who violate their rights).[172]

The DTSA would create a private cause of action in federal courts for trade secret owners to sue misappropriators. The DTSA would establish the new private right of action by rewriting the provision of the EEA that currently authorizes the Attorney General to bring a civil action to obtain "appropriate injunctive relief" against any violation of the EEA, codified at 18 U.S.C. Section 1836. However, the changes proposed by the DTSA would amend Section 1836 to omit the Attorney General's power to initiate civil proceedings to enjoin violations. It is unclear whether the sponsors of the bill intended this outcome or whether it is an inadvertent oversight in legislative drafting.

The DTSA would allow an owner of a trade secret to bring a private civil action if the person is aggrieved by either of the two primary offenses under the EEA: 18 U.S.C. Section 1831(a) (economic espionage) or Section 1832(a) (theft of trade secrets).[173] The trade secret owner would also have the right to file a lawsuit if the owner suffers a misappropriation of a trade secret that is related to a product or service used in, or intended for use in, interstate or foreign commerce.[174] The legislation would amend the EEA's definition section (18 U.S.C. Section 1839) to include

---

[169] 160 CONG. REC. S3297 (daily ed. May 22, 2014) (statement of Sen. Levin).

[170] S. 2384, §2(a).

[171] *Id.* §2(b).

[172] News Release, *Senator Coons, Hatch Introduce Bill to Combat Theft of Trade Secrets and Protect Jobs,* April 29, 2014.

[173] S. 2267, §2(a), adding new 18 U.S.C. §1836(a)(1)(A).

[174] *Id.* §2(a), adding new 18 U.S.C. §1836(a)(1)(B).

definitions of the terms "misappropriation" and "improper means" that closely mirror those found in the FAIR Act.[175]

Similar to the FAIR Act, the DTSA would provide a court with the power to issue civil ex parte orders for the preservation of evidence and the seizure of any property used, in any manner or part, to commit or facilitate the commission of a violation of the EEA.[176] The DTSA includes a few conditions that would limit the scope of the seizure order, including that the order may not allow the "seizure of any property that is merely incidental to the alleged violation unless necessary to preserve evidence," and that the order "shall provide for the seizure of any property in a manner that, to the extent possible, does not interrupt normal and legitimate business operations unrelated to the trade secret."[177] The DTSA would also adopt the same procedural requirements for ex parte applications for seizure orders as the ones that currently govern the seizure of goods and counterfeit trademarks under the Trademark Act of 1946 (15 U.S.C. Section 1116).[178]

The legislation would empower a court to offer similar remedies for trade secret misappropriation as those proposed by the FAIR Act, including injunctive relief, damages, punitive damages of up to 3 times the amount of damages (note that the FAIR Act would cap exemplary damage awards to an amount not more than 2 times the damages amount), and reasonable attorney's fees. Unlike the FAIR Act's three-year statute of limitations, the DTSA would establish a five-year limitations period.

Finally, the DTSA includes a "rule of construction" provision[179] that declares that nothing in the DTSA shall be construed (1) to preempt any other provision of law or (2) to modify the EEA's existing rule of construction (codified at 18 U.S.C. Section 1838) stating that the EEA does not preempt or displace any civil or criminal remedies provided by federal or state law for the misappropriation of a trade secret.

H.Res. 643, Calling for Further Defense Against the People's Republic of China's State-sponsored Cyber-enabled Theft of Trade Secrets

Introduced by Representative Chabot, this House resolution calls on

1. the President to aggressively implement and coordinate the Strategy on Mitigating the Theft of United States Trade Secrets;

2. the People's Republic of China (PRC) to end the practice of cyber-enabled espionage against U.S. firms and to cooperate in cybersecurity efforts with the United States;

---

[175] *Id.* §2(b), amending 18 U.S.C. §1839. Note that the EEA's definition section already includes an expansive definition of "trade secret" as well as "owner" (includes a person or entity).

[176] *Id.* §2(a), adding new 18 U.S.C. §1836(a)(2).

[177] *Id.* §2(a), adding new 18 U.S.C. §1836(a)(2)(A)(ii).

[178] *Id.* §2(a), adding new 18 U.S.C. §1836(a)(2)(B).

[179] *Id.* §2(e).

3. the Department of Justice to advance investigations into cyber espionage by actors originating in the PRC;

4. the U.S. government to condemn cyber-enabled espionage for the purposes of stealing intellectual property and trade secrets, pursue counter intelligence capacities, and prosecute such individuals should they enter U.S. territory;

5. the U.S. Trade Representative to estimate the loss from cyber theft, compile a list of actors that cause the most damage to U.S. firms, and pursue a dispute settlement case at the World Trade Organization;

6. the U.S. Office of the National Counterintelligence Executive to update the unclassified report to Congress on Foreign Economic Collection and Industrial Espionage in 2009-2011;

7. the Department of Defense (DOD) to restrict military-to-military contacts with the People's Liberation Army;

8. the Federal Bureau of Investigation and the Department of Homeland Security to expand warnings to U.S. companies about the large array of tools used by actors originating in the PRC to illicit trade secrets;

9. the DOD and the Department of State to provide briefings of the U.S.-China cybersecurity working group meetings in 2013; and

10. Federal departments and agencies to expand cooperation with allies and partners to better coordinate defense against cyber threats.

H.R. 5103, Chinese Communist Economic Espionage Sanctions Act

The Chinese Communist Economic Espionage Sanctions Act, introduced by Representative Rohrabacher, expresses the sense of Congress that the Chinese Communist Party and the China government should be condemned for conducting cyber and economic espionage against the United States.[180] The act also calls for the freezing of assets of certain Chinese entities and persons as well as denying them admission into the United States. Section 4(a) of the act would require the President to block and prohibit all transactions in property and property interests of a "covered Chinese state-owned enterprise" or a person who is a member of the board of directors, an executive officer, or a senior official of such enterprise, if those property and property interests are in the United States, come within the United States, or are within the possession or control of a U.S. person.[181] The legislation defines "covered Chinese state-owned enterprise" to mean an enterprise that "(A) is organized under the laws of the People's Republic of China, including a foreign branch of such enterprise; and (B) is owned or controlled by the Government of the People's Republic of China or the Chinese Communist Party."[182] The act would make an alien ineligible to receive a visa and ineligible for U.S. admission if the alien is a member of the board of directors, an executive officer, or a senior official of a covered Chinese state-owned enterprise.[183] Finally, the act would direct the Secretary of State to revoke the visa or other documentation of any alien who would be ineligible to receive the visa or documentation as a

---

[180] H.R. 5103, §3.

[181] *Id.* §4(a).

[182] *Id.* §4(d)(1).

[183] *Id.* §5(a).

result of the act.[184] (These immigration-related consequences are similar to those proposed in H.R. 2281, the Cyber Economic Espionage Accountability Act, described above.)

H.R. 5233, Trade Secrets Protection Act of 2014

Introduced by Representative Holding on July 29, 2014, the Trade Secrets Protection Act of 2014 is a companion bill to S. 2267, the Defend Trade Secrets Act (DTSA) of 2014. While substantially similar in many respects to the Senate bill, there also are several significant differences, as described below.

Like the DTSA, H.R. 5233 would amend the civil proceedings section of the EEA (18 U.S.C. Section 1836) to provide a trade secret owner with the right to bring a federal civil action to obtain injunctive and monetary relief "if the person is aggrieved by a misappropriation of a trade secret that is related to a product or service used in, or intended for use in, interstate or foreign commerce."[185] However, unlike the DTSA that entirely rewrites Section 1836 and—perhaps due to an unintentional drafting error—*omits* the current statutory provision that authorizes the Attorney General to initiate civil proceedings to enjoin violations, H.R. 5233 would amend 18 U.S.C. Section 1836 by inserting the new private civil action as subsection (b) and would leave unchanged the original subsection (a) that pertains to the Attorney General's power to seek injunctive relief in a civil action.

H.R. 5233 also contains several provisions that were included in response[186] to concerns raised about seizure provisions included in previously introduced legislation, including the DTSA and the FAIR Act. As previously described, the DTSA would allow a court to issue an order, based on an ex parte motion, to preserve evidence and seize any property used, in any manner or part, to commit or facilitate the commission of a violation of the EEA. One of the witnesses at a House Judiciary subcommittee hearing held in June 2014 explained that while his company supported the establishment of a robust federal trade secrets law, he was worried that this seizure remedy was overbroad and that it might harm property owned by "innocent third parties" such as his company that hosts its customers' data in the Internet "cloud":

> salesforce.com relies on the Internet to provide a variety of software as a service. ... Our customers' data and our software are stored in large storage arrays that we call pods. ... Individual customer data at the physical level is intermixed with data of other customers according to complex algorithms that take into account workloads, access speed and security. While an individual customer's data may be arrayed across dozens or hundreds of storage devices intermixed with others' data, no customer has the ability to access the other customer's data without that customer's permission. ...
>
> The problem with the seizure provisions included in many proposals we have seen for a federal trade secret law is they do not take into account this new and increasingly common way of doing business over the Internet. Rather, all of the proposals are based off of normal seizure rules in trademark counterfeiting statutes and copyright statutes and in Federal Rule of Civil Procedure 65. These rules and statutes were originally drafted before there was an

---

[184] *Id.* §5(b).

[185] H.R. 5233, §2(a), *adding new* 18 U.S.C. §1836(b)(1).

[186] Tamlin Bason, *House Trade Secret Bill Tightens Seizure Standards Relative to Counterpart Senate Bill*, BNA'S PATENT, TRADEMARK & COPYRIGHT JOURNAL, July 30, 2014 (citing a spokesperson for Democratic Members of the House Judiciary Committee).

Internet and, in some instances, were first drafted when computer disk drives had not even been invented.[187]

H.R. 5233 includes a narrower seizure provision that contains several provisions intended to address this alleged problem in the DTSA. Specifically, the legislation would allow a seizure order to issue only if the court finds that the following statements are correct:[188]

1. an order issued pursuant to Rule 65(b) of the Federal Rules of Civil Procedure (authorizing temporary restraining order) would be inadequate because the party to which the order would be issued would evade, avoid, or otherwise not comply with such an order;

2. an immediate and irreparable injury will occur if such seizure is not ordered;

3. the harm to the applicant of denying the application outweighs the harm to the legitimate interests of the person against whom seizure would be ordered if granting the application and substantially outweighs the harm to any third parties who may be harmed by such seizure;

4. the applicant is likely to succeed in showing that the person against whom seizure would be ordered misappropriated the trade secret and is in possession of the trade secret;

5. the application describes with reasonable particularity the matter to be seized and, to the extent reasonable under the circumstances, identifies the location where the matter is to be seized;

6. the person against whom seizure would be ordered, or persons acting in concert with such person, would destroy, move, hide, or otherwise make such matter inaccessible to the court, if the applicant were to proceed on notice to such person; and

7. the applicant has not publicized the requested seizure.

In addition, H.R. 5233 would require that any such seizure order "minimizes any interruption of the business operations of third parties and, to the extent possible, does not interrupt those legitimate business operations of the person accused of misappropriating the trade secret that are unrelated to the trade secret that has allegedly been misappropriated."[189] In addition, H.R. 5233 would establish a cause of action against the seizure order applicant for anyone who suffers damage caused by wrongful or excessive seizure.[190]

Observers have praised the inclusion of these safeguard measures in H.R. 5233, stating that,

> These protections are as important to the legislation as the ability to obtain a seizure order. The protections will prevent fishing expeditions. They will also ensure that a third party that

---

[187] *Trade Secrets: Promoting and Protecting American Innovation, Competitiveness and Market Access in Foreign Markets: Hearings Before the House Judiciary Comm., Subcomm. on Courts, Intellectual Property and Internet*, 113th Cong. 2d Sess. (2014) (statement of David M. Simon, Senior Vice President, salesforce.com, Inc.), at 5-6 (citations omitted).

[188] H.R. 5233, §2(a), *adding new* 18 U.S.C. §1836(b)(2)(A)(ii).

[189] *Id.* §2(a), *adding new* 18 U.S.C. §1836(b)(2)(B)(ii).

[190] *Id.* §2(a), *adding new* 18 U.S.C. §1836(b)(2)(F).

is not involved in the misappropriation but has an allegedly misappropriated trade secret residing on its server will not be subject to a seizure order.[191]

Author Contact Information

Brian T. Yeh
Legislative Attorney
byeh@crs.loc.gov, 7-5182

---

[191] Richard Hertling et al., *Inside The House's New Trade Secrets Bill,* Law360.com, August 6, 2014, *available at* http://www.cov.com/files/Publication/63376dda-d9fb-44be-9540-26892650b40e/Presentation/PublicationAttachment/ 9d94d9eb-face-40f6-9e67-380e8786c04c/Law360_Inside_The_Houses_New_Trade_Secrets_Bill.pdf.